KINDERGA

Bible Bulletin Boards

Written by Carolyn Larsen

Illustrated by Carol Tiernon

Cover Illustrated by Judy Hierstein

A Division of Frank Schaffer Publications, Inc.
23740 Hawthorne Blvd., Torrance, CA 90505

Table of Contents

To Teachers and Parents

Bible Bulletin Boards is a wonderful way to let children have a great time learning all about God and His Word and Christian concepts and values! It includes a fantastic variety of bulletin boards that have been designed to teach children some valuable lessons and important skills. Choose from themes featuring holidays, Bible stories, memory verses, and so much more.

Each bulletin board idea features at least one title suggestion, a Bible verse, a list of materials needed, simple directions for assembly, any necessary patterns, and suggestions of ways to share the board with the children.

The children will have a great time learning all about Jesus' resurrection, Samson, Moses, the disciples, the fruits of the Spirit, some miracles Jesus performed, and so much more. In addition, they will be practicing skills like coloring, cutting, pasting, critical thinking, and analyzing, among many others.

Fantastic Freedom

Give thanks to the Lord, call on his name; make known among the nations what he has done.
(1 Chronicles 16:8)

This board is fun to do to teach the children about Independence Day and the wonderful freedoms we all enjoy and should thank God for.

Materials Needed:

one enlarged copy of the broken firecracker pattern on page 5, one copy of the firecracker and streamer patterns on page 6 per child, crayons or markers, scissors

Preparation:

Color the broken firecracker pattern and attach it to the center of the board. Attach the title, too.

Directions:

Give each child a streamer to decorate using crayons or markers. When they are finished, curl each streamer with scissors and attach them to the board as shown. Next, help each child write or draw a picture of something for which he or she is thankful on the firecracker pattern. Attach them all over the board.

Fantastic Freedom

continued

Fantastic Freedom

continued

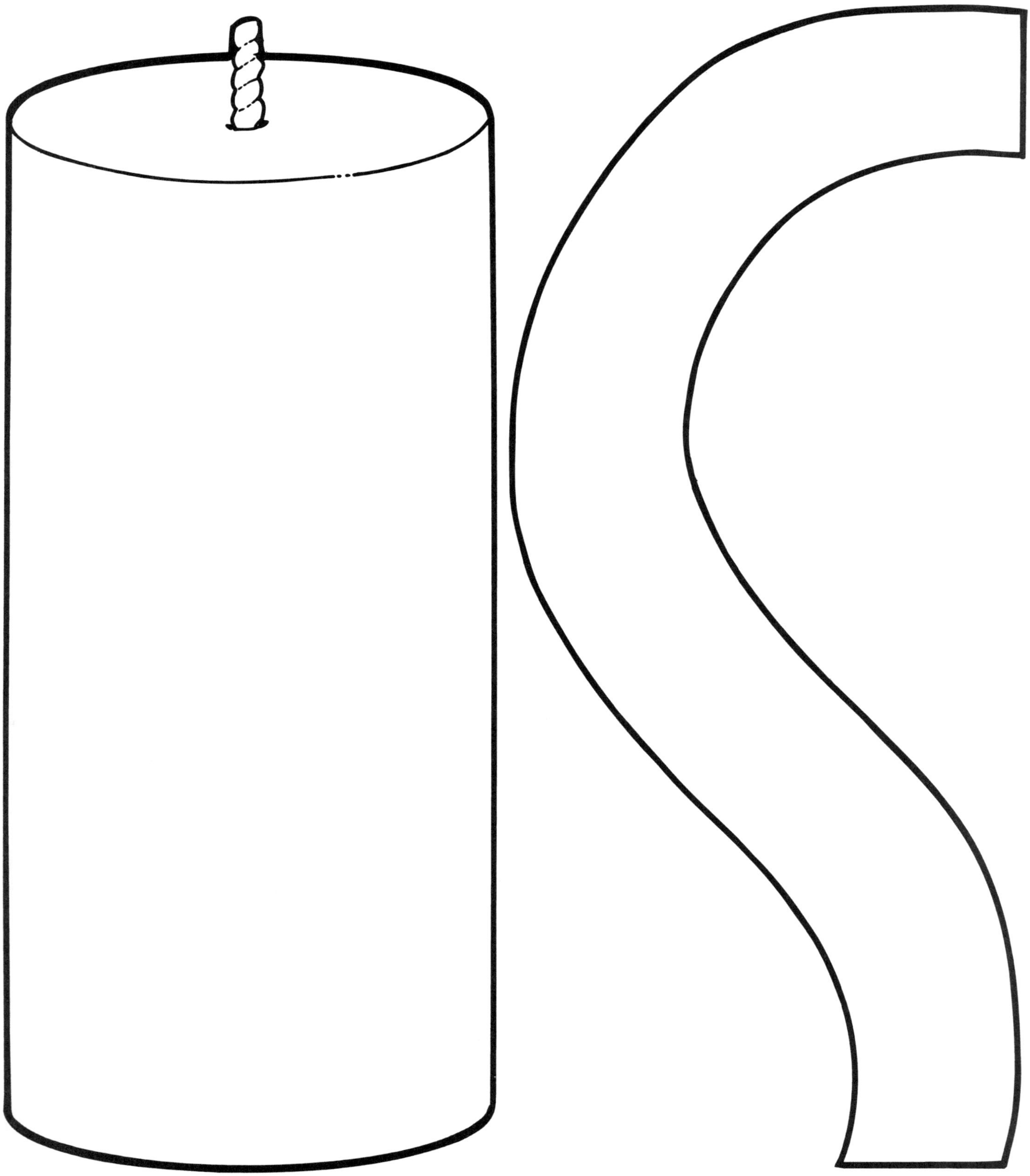

Happy Birthday

I praise you because I am fearfully and wonderfully made . . . (Psalm 139:14)

This board is a great way to celebrate each child's special qualities!

Materials Needed:

one enlarged copy of the present pattern on page 8; one copy of the present pattern on page 9 per child; scissors; crayons, markers, glue, glitter, and other decorative items; one sheet of white paper per child (same size as present pattern), stapler (optional: photo of each child)

Preparation:

Decorate and attach the enlarged present and the title to the board.

Directions:

Let the children decorate their present patterns using markers, crayons, glitter, or any other supplies you have available. Once they have finished, attach each decorated piece to a white piece of paper, cut to the same size as the pattern. Fold each pattern on the dotted line, and staple it to the white paper so that the present art can be lifted up to reveal what is inside the package. On each piece of white paper, write the appropriate child's name and birthdate, and have him or her help you finish this sentence: "I am special because ________." You may also tape each child's picture on this sheet.

Happy Birthday

continued

Happy Birthday

continued

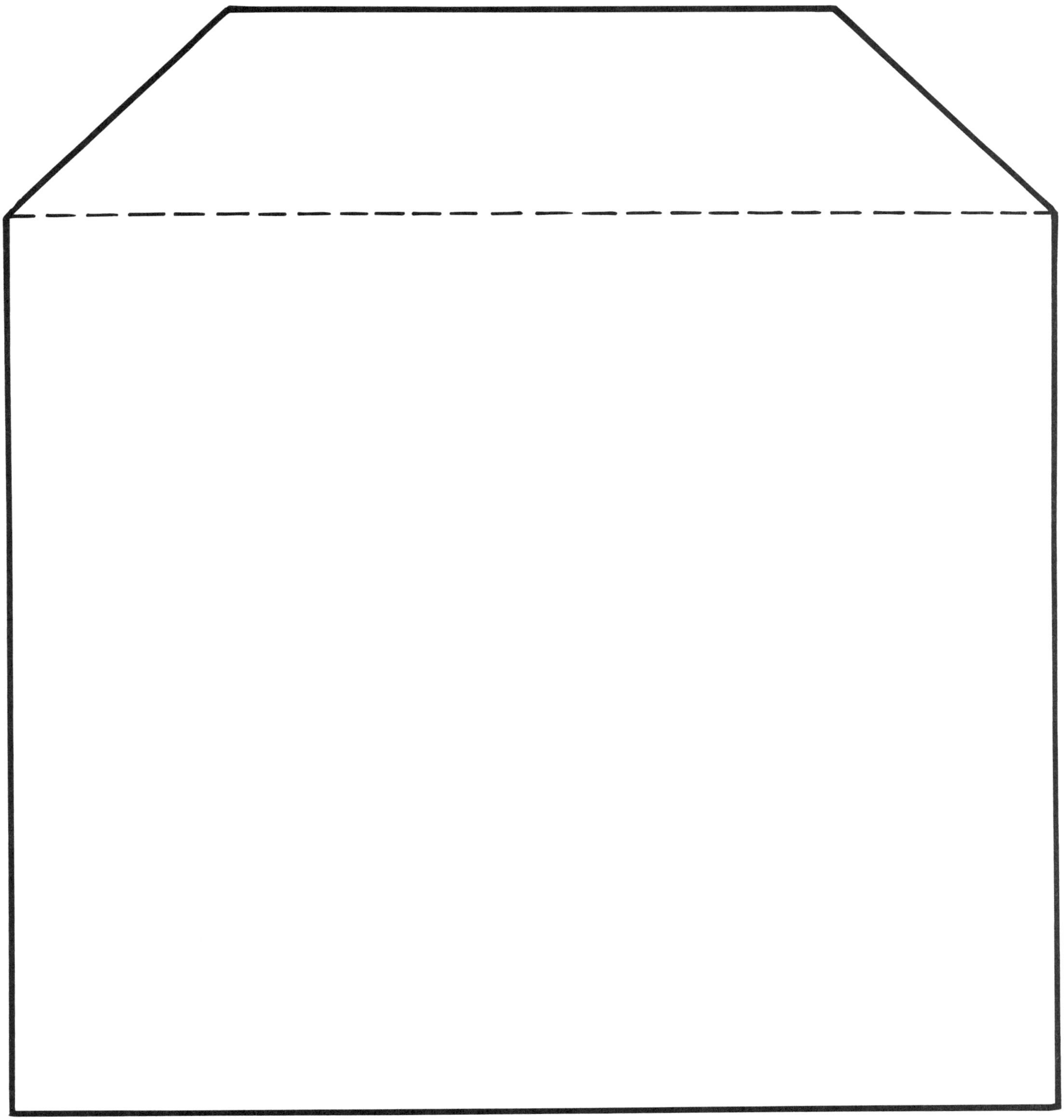

Give Thanks

Let us come before him with thanksgiving. (Psalm 95:2)

This board will help the children remember to thank God for all that He has given them.

Materials Needed:

one copy of the turkey pattern on page 11 per child, one copy of the feet and feather patterns on page 12 per child, crayons or markers, stapler or tape

Preparation:

Attach the title to the board.

Directions:

Give each child a turkey, feet, and some feather patterns. Have the children color their turkeys. Help them think of things they are thankful for and write one item on each feather. Then let the children lightly color their feathers. Staple or tape the feathers onto each child's turkey and then to the board.

Give Thanks

continued

Give Thanks

continued

Happy Mother's Day

"Honor your . . . mother . . ." (Exodus 20:12)

What a great board to remind children how wonderful mothers are!

Materials Needed:
one pastel colored cupcake liner per child, a picture of each child, green construction paper, two green construction paper leaves per child (see pattern to the right), tape or glue, stapler

Preparation:
Attach the title to the board. Tape or glue a picture of each child inside a cupcake liner. Staple the cupcake liners to the board. Cut stems from construction paper and attach one to each flower.

Directions:
Give each child two leaves. Ask the children to think of two things they especially appreciate about their mothers. Help them write those things on their leaves and staple them to the appropriate flowers. Talk about ways they can honor their mothers.

Merry Christmas

"Today . . . a Savior has been born to you; he is Christ the Lord." (Luke 2:11)

With so much emphasis on gifts at Christmas, this board is the perfect way to remind the children of the best Christmas present of all!

Materials Needed:

an enlarged copy of the patterns on page 15, one copy of one of the ornament patterns on page 16 per child, blue paper (board background), crayons or markers (optional: glitter and glue, colored cellophane, copies of the present patterns on pages 8 and 9, enlarged copies of the manger and baby Jesus patterns on page 19, an enlarged copy of the star pattern on page 20)

Preparation:

Cover the board with blue paper. Attach the title, Christmas tree, trunk, and star to the board. Wrap cellophane around the trunk to resemble a tree skirt, if desired. Add decorated present patterns and baby Jesus, star, and manger patterns to create a more complex board.

Directions:

Let each child decorate an ornament using crayons or markers (and glitter and glue if provided). Then "hang" the ornaments on the tree. Discuss with the children the fact that God loved us so much that He sent Jesus to earth as a baby.

Merry Christmas

continued

Merry Christmas

continued

Away in a Manger

". . . You will find a baby wrapped in cloths and lying in a manger." (Luke 2:12)

This board provides a wonderful way to explain the birth of Jesus to the children.

Materials Needed:
dark blue paper (board background), enlarged copies of the patterns on pages 18–20, crayons or markers (optional: hay)

Preparation:
Cover the board with dark blue paper. Color the patterns and cut them out. Attach the title.

Directions:
Tell the children the story of Jesus' birth (Luke 2:1–20). Then attach the manger scene to the board, one piece at a time, explaining the significance of each character in the story of the birth of Jesus. If possible, put some real hay inside the manger before the baby is added.

Away in a Manger

continued

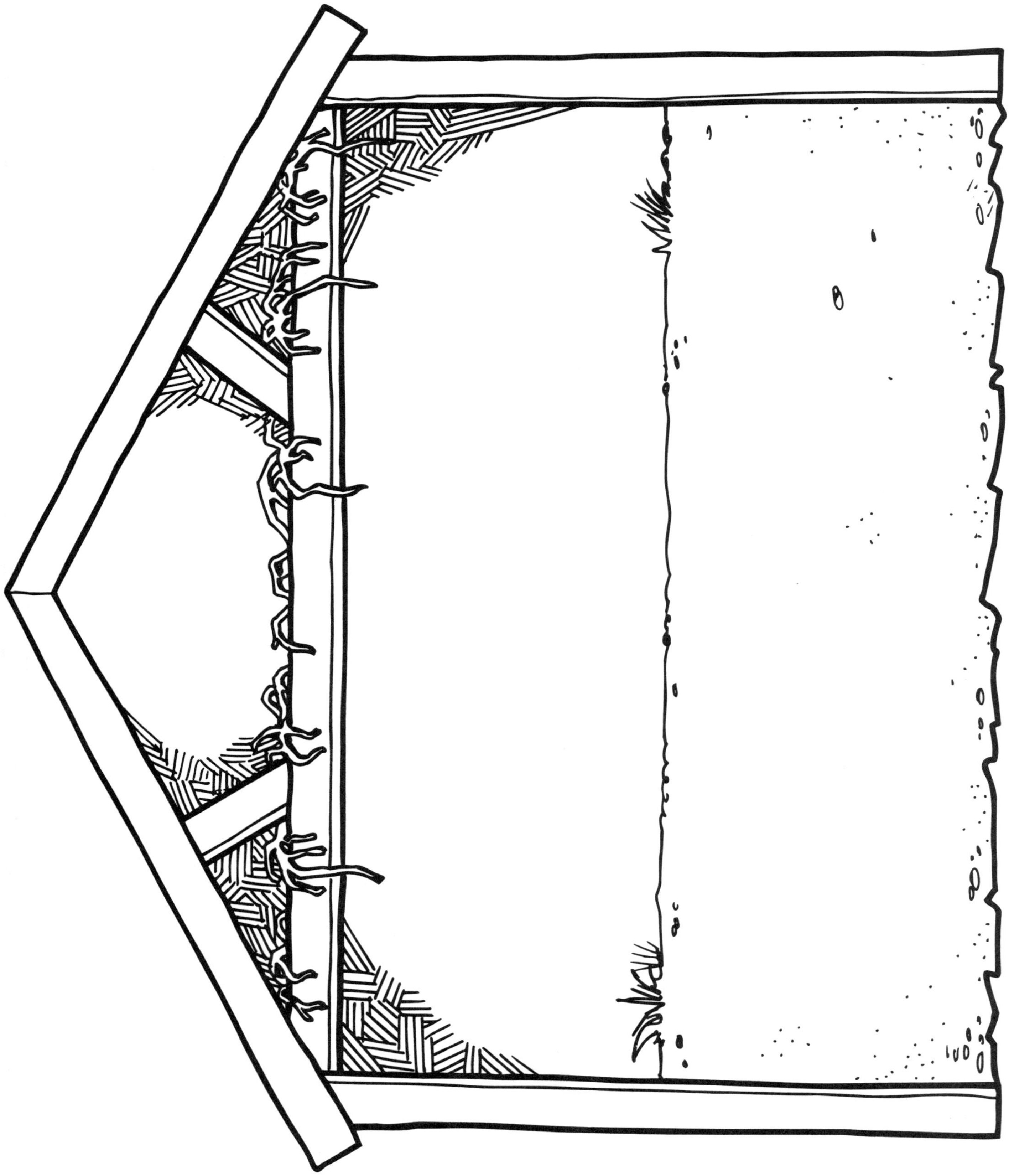

Away in a Manger

continued

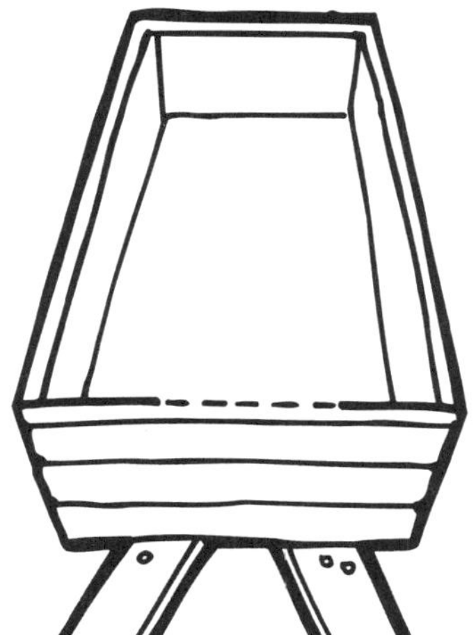

Away in a Manger

continued

He Is Risen!

"He is not here; he has risen! . . ." (Luke 24:6)

This board is a fun way for children to learn about Jesus' resurrection (Luke 24:1–12).

Materials Needed:

an enlarged copy of the tomb, stone, and tree patterns on pages 22–23, many colors of construction paper, crayons or markers, 2 straight pins

Preparation:

Attach the title to the board. Add green construction paper grass. Then staple the tomb and the tree to the board. Next, attach the stone to the board using two straight pins, one on either side. This enables you to "roll the stone away" and show the empty tomb.

Directions:

Provide the children with a variety of colored construction paper. Help them create flowers to attach to the board. (You could provide round circles and petal shapes to help them assemble flowers. Or, you could just draw and color flowers on the board with the children's help.) Tell the story of Jesus' resurrection. Then have the children act out this story. Or, greet the children with "He is risen." They can respond with "He is risen indeed!"

He Is Risen!

continued

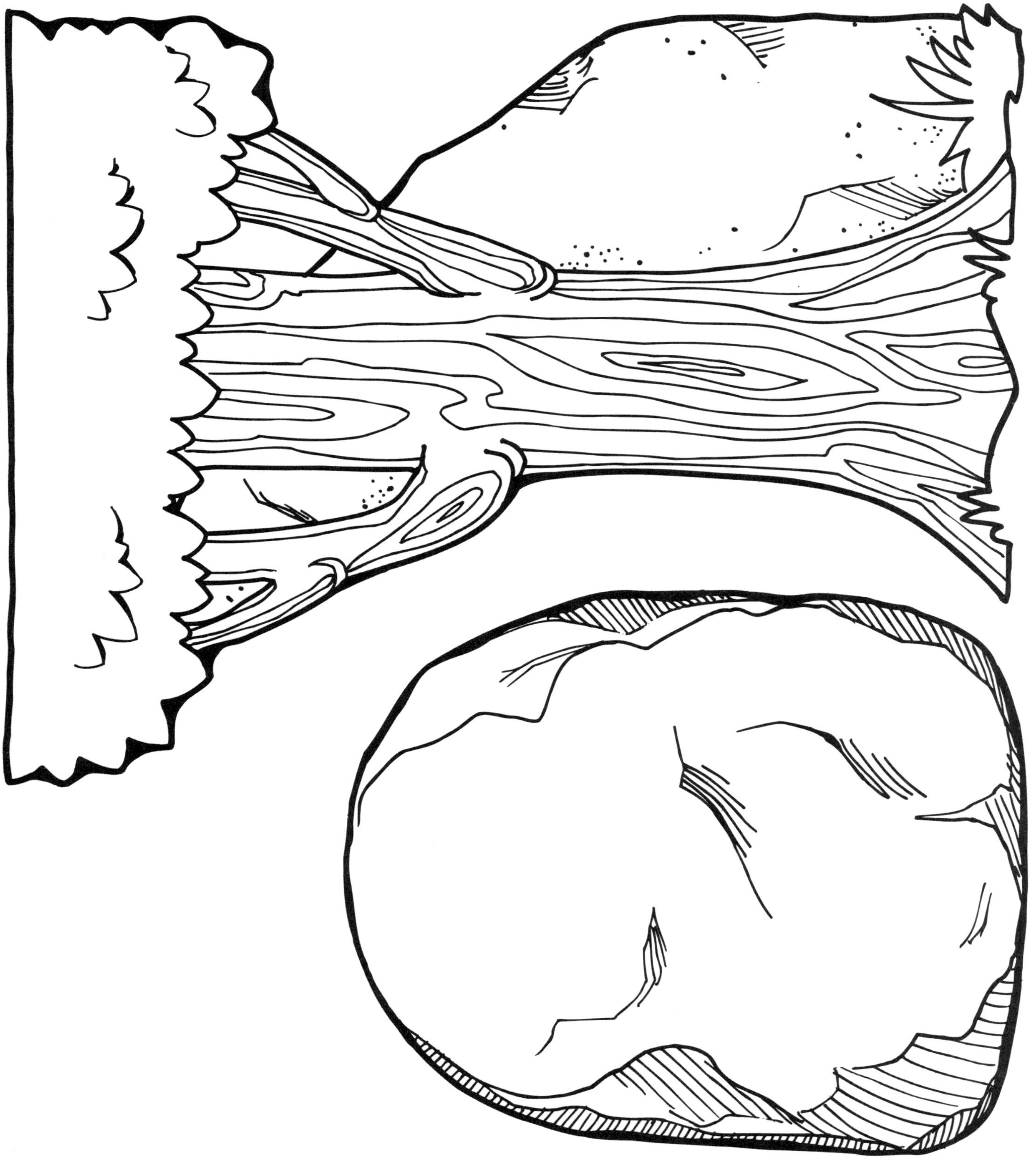

He Is Risen!

continued

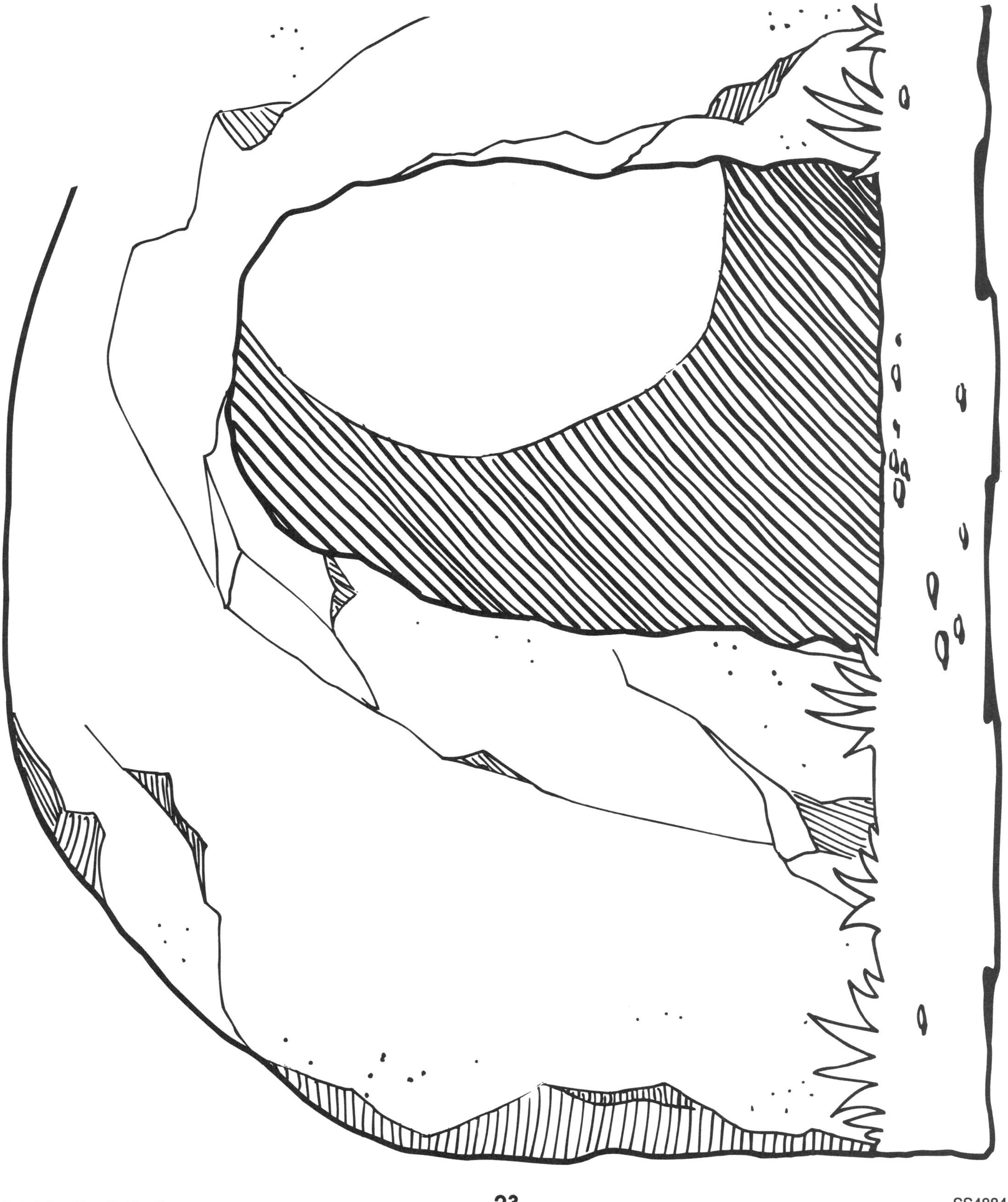

Love One Another

. . . love one another as he commanded us. (1 John 3:23)

This board is a great way to remind the children of all the people they love!

Materials Needed:
copies of the heart patterns on this page and page 25 on red paper, white paper (board background)

Preparation:
Cover the board with white paper. Attach the title. Scatter the red hearts all over the board as shown.

Directions:
Ask each child to name someone he or she loves. Write the names on the hearts. Let the children name as many people as they desire.

Love One Another

continued

Thank God for Dads!

A wise son heeds his father's instruction . . . (Proverbs 13:1)

What a fun board to do to help children appreciate dear old dad!

Materials Needed:

one copy of the necktie pattern on page 27 per child, one enlarged copy of the "Thank God for Dads" pattern on page 27, brightly colored paper (board background), crayons or markers, stapler

Preparation:

Cover the board with the brightly colored paper. Staple the enlarged "Thank God for Dads" pattern to the center of the board.

Directions:

Give each child a necktie to decorate using crayons or markers. Then staple the neckties randomly around the board. Let each child tell one thing he or she likes to do with his or her dad.

Thank God for Dads!

continued

Zacchaeus, You Come Down!

. . . *"Zacchaeus, come down immediately. I must stay at your house today."* (Luke 19:5)

This board is a fun way to teach the children that Jesus befriended all people—even sinners.

Materials Needed:
brown construction paper, a copy of the Zacchaeus pattern on page 29, many copies of the leaf patterns on page 29 on green construction paper, stapler

Preparation:
Use the brown construction paper to create a large tree with branches. Staple it to the board. Color Zacchaeus and staple him to the board. Attach the title.

Directions:
Read or tell the children the story of Zacchaeus (Luke 19:1–10). Discuss it with the children. Then let the children cut out copies of the leaves. Staple them all over the tree branches and around Zacchaeus.

Zacchaeus, You Come Down!

continued

A Broken Promise

". . . O God, please strengthen me just once more . . ." (Judges 16:28)

Children love the story of Samson, and this board is a fun way to teach them all about it.

Materials Needed:

an enlarged copy of the scissors pattern on page 31, one copy of the scissors pattern per child, several 8" pieces of black yarn, brightly colored paper (board background)

Preparation:

Cover the board with brightly colored paper. Attach the title.

Directions:

As you attach the enlarged pair of scissors and the "hair" to the board, tell the children the story of how Samson broke his promise (Judges 16). Then let the children dictate or write promises they make to God on their scissors. Attach them to the board.

A Broken Promise

continued

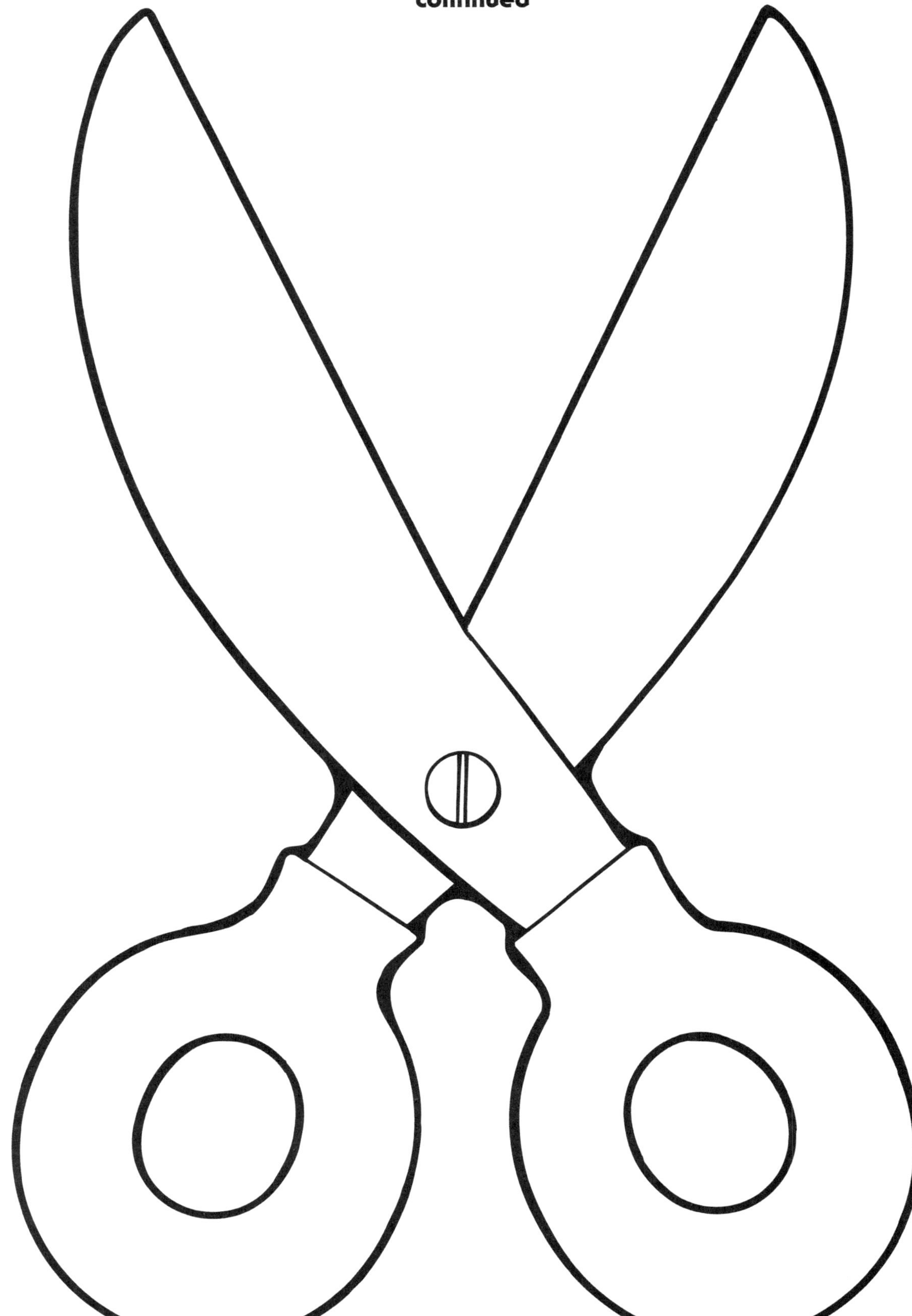

In the Beginning

. . . And God saw that it was good. (Genesis 1:12)

The story of Creation is fascinating to children. They will love this board!

Materials Needed:

enlarged copies of the patterns on pages 33–34, markers, seven white 3" x 5" cards

Preparation:

Use markers to color the world pattern to look like a globe. Write what God created on each day on each 3" x 5" card (Day 1—light; Day 2—sky; Day 3—plants; Day 4—sun, moon, and stars; Day 5—fish and birds; Day 6—animals and man; Day 7—God rested.). Attach the globe and the cards to the board as shown.

Directions:

Explain to the children what God created each day. Read the story of Creation to the children (Genesis 1). Talk about how wonderful God's creation is and how His creation shows His love for us. Add the patterns to the board as you discuss each day of creation. (You could give each child a star to decorate to add to the background.)

In the Beginning

continued

In the Beginning

continued

Jonah and the Big Fish

". . . I called to the Lord and he answered me . . ." (Jonah 2:2)

The story of Jonah is a favorite of many children. They are sure to love this board!

Materials Needed:
dark blue paper (board background), an enlarged copy of the pattern on page 36, a copy of Jonah on page 37, one copy of a fish pattern on page 37 per child, crayons or markers

Preparation:
Cover the board with dark blue paper. Write the Bible verse and title. (The title can be added on a light blue piece of paper with scallops cut along the bottom to represent waves.) Color the enlarged fish and Jonah patterns. Attach the fish to the board and then attach Jonah in the center.

Directions:
Tell the children the story of Jonah and the giant fish (Jonah 1–3). Discuss obeying God with them. Also discuss how God answered Jonah's prayers and how He can answer our prayers, too. Let each child color a fish. Randomly attach them to the board.

Jonah and the Big Fish

continued

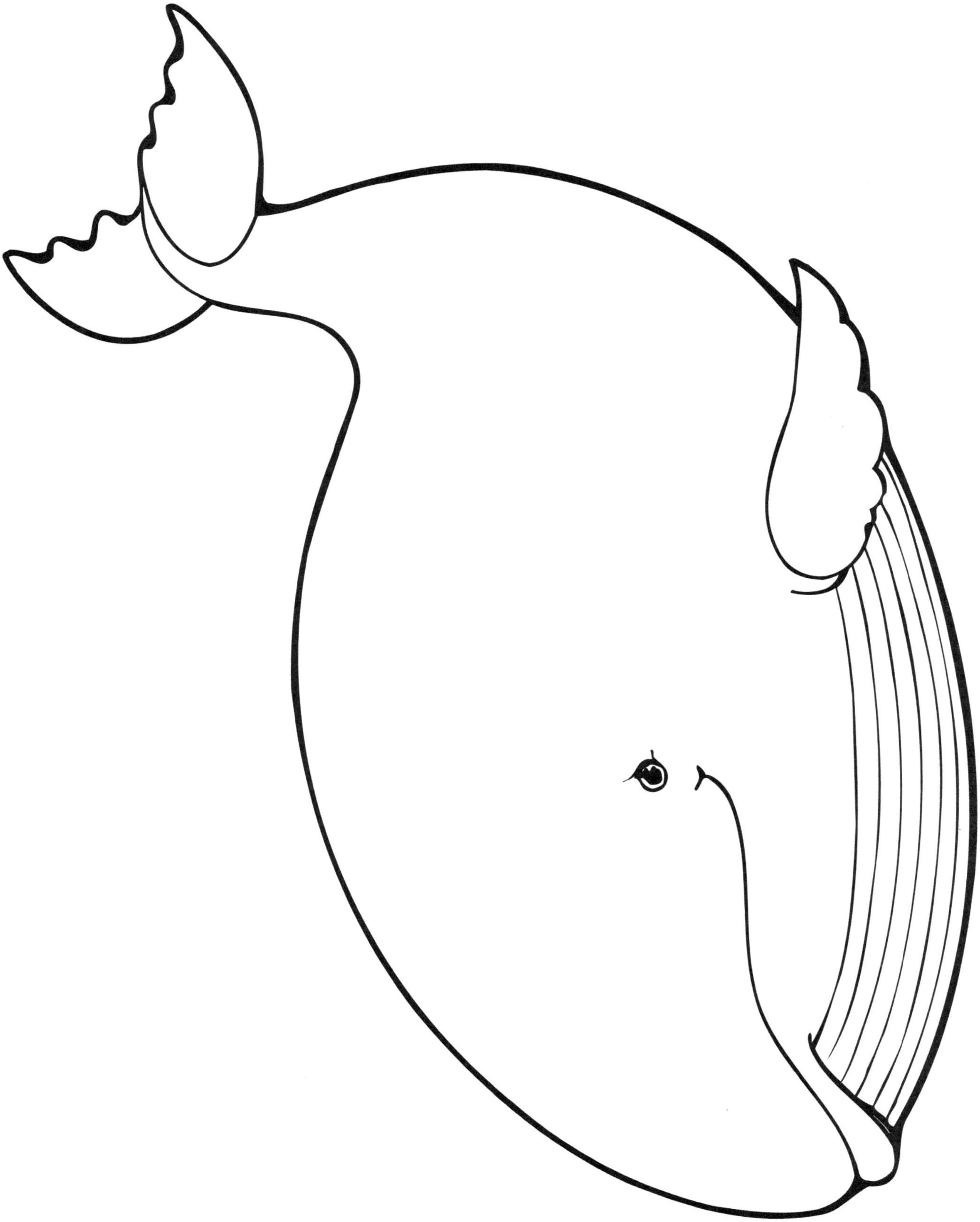

Jonah and the Big Fish

continued

God Will Protect Me

I can do everything through him who gives me strength. (Philippians 4:13)

This board is a great way to teach children the well-loved story of David and Goliath.

Materials Needed:
an enlarged copy of the patterns on pages 39–40, crayons or markers, brown or gray "rocks" cut out of construction paper

Directions:
Color the pictures of Goliath's legs and David shooting his sling. Cut them out and staple them and the "rocks" to the board. Tell the children the story of David and Goliath (1 Samuel 17). Discuss with them how God protects them and can make them strong Christians.

God Will Protect Me

continued

God Will Protect Me

continued

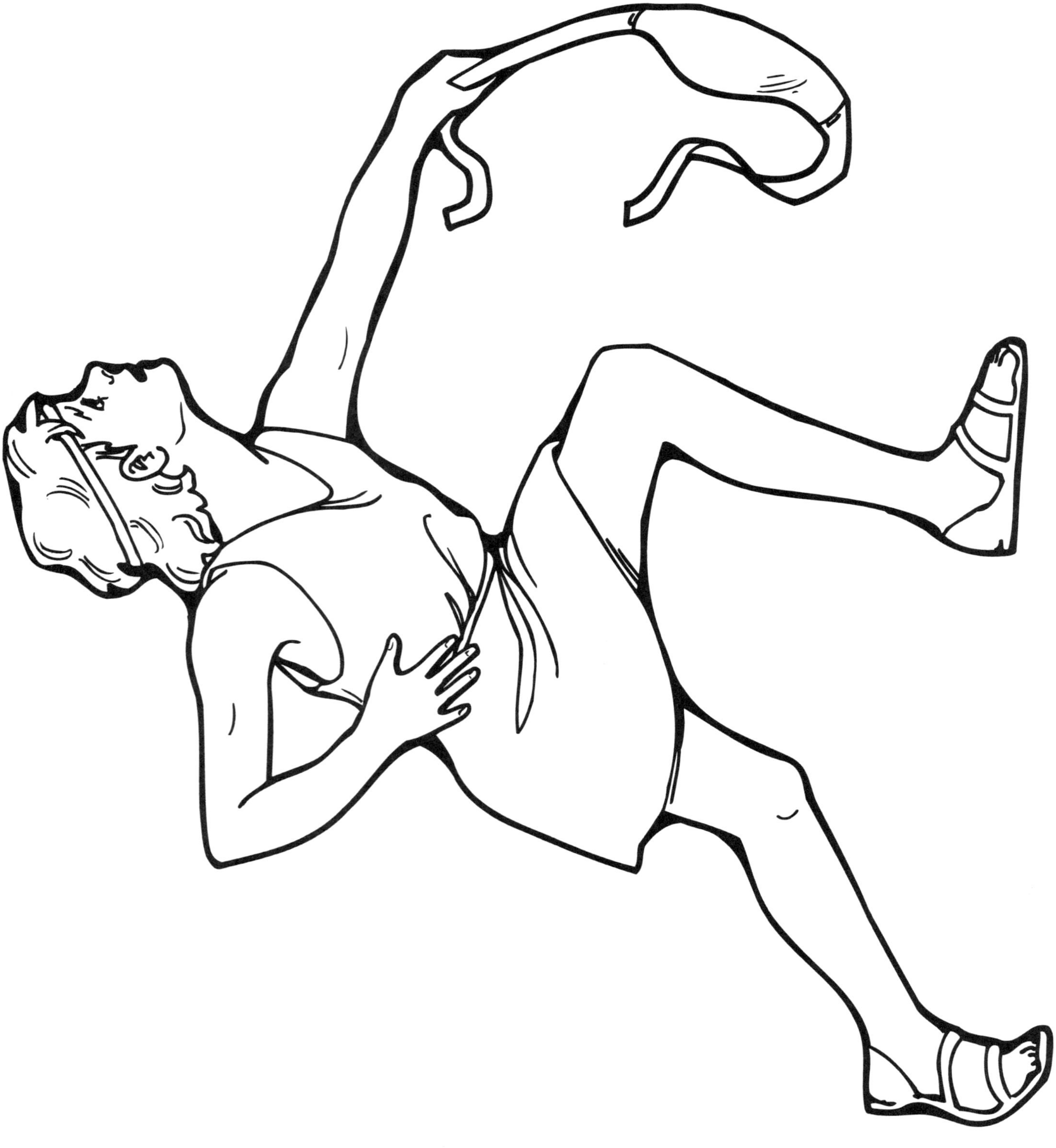

Walking on Water

. . . *"It is I; don't be afraid."* (John 6:20)

This board is a great way to teach the children about Jesus' power.

Materials Needed:
an enlarged copy of the Jesus pattern on page 42, one copy of one of the fish patterns on page 43 per child, 2 colors of blue paper (board background), crayons or markers, glitter, glue

Preparation:
Cover the board with a different shade of blue paper than the waves will be. To create waves, take sheets of blue construction paper and cut as shown. Staple the figure of Jesus to the center of the board between the waves.

Directions:
Give each child a fish to decorate using crayons or markers and glitter. Tell them the story of Jesus walking on the water (John 6:16–24). Discuss His power and His love for His disciples. Staple the children's fish among the waves.

Walking on Water

continued

Walking on Water

continued

An Arkful of Animals

Noah did everything just as God commanded him. (Genesis 6:22)

The story of Noah's Ark is a favorite of many children. They will love this bulletin board, too!

Materials Needed:

enlarged copies of the patterns on pages 45–48, green and blue paper (board background), crayons or markers

Preparation:

Cover the board with green and blue paper and attach the ark and the title to the board. (Note: You will be adding a rainbow to the top of this board in the bulletin board idea on page 49.)

Directions:

Let the children color the animals. Attach the animals and Noah to and around the ark as you tell the story of how God spoke to Noah and warned him about the coming flood (Genesis 6:1–7:24). Remind the children that God protected Noah because he had honored and obeyed God. Talk about ways they can obey God.

An Arkful of Animals

continued

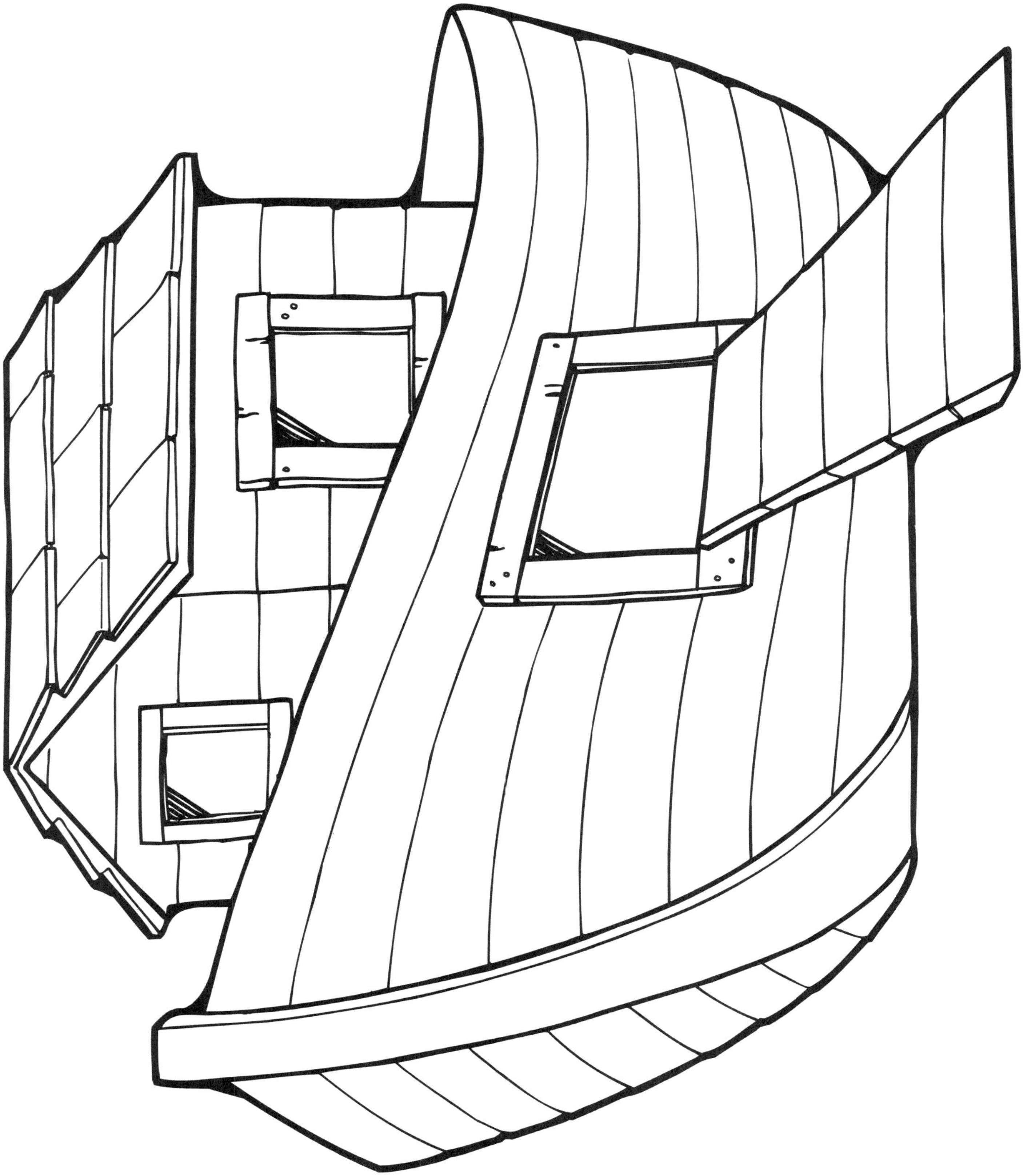

An Arkful of Animals

continued

An Arkful of Animals

continued

An Arkful of Animals

continued

The Rainbow Promise

"I have set my rainbow in the clouds, and it will be the sign of the covenant between me and the earth." (Genesis 9:13)

This board is a great way to teach the children about the promise God made to us.

Materials Needed:
two enlarged copies of the rainbow pattern on page 50 (large enough to stretch from end to end on the board), an enlarged copy of the sun pattern on page 50, the completed bulletin board as described on page 44, crayons or markers

Preparation:
This board should still have Noah's ark and the animals on it from the board described on page 44. Be sure to add the new title.

Directions:
Tell the children the story of how God saved Noah and instructed Noah and his family to have children and fill the earth again (Genesis 8:1–9:17). As you talk, attach the rainbow and the sun to the board above the ark.

The Rainbow Promise

continued

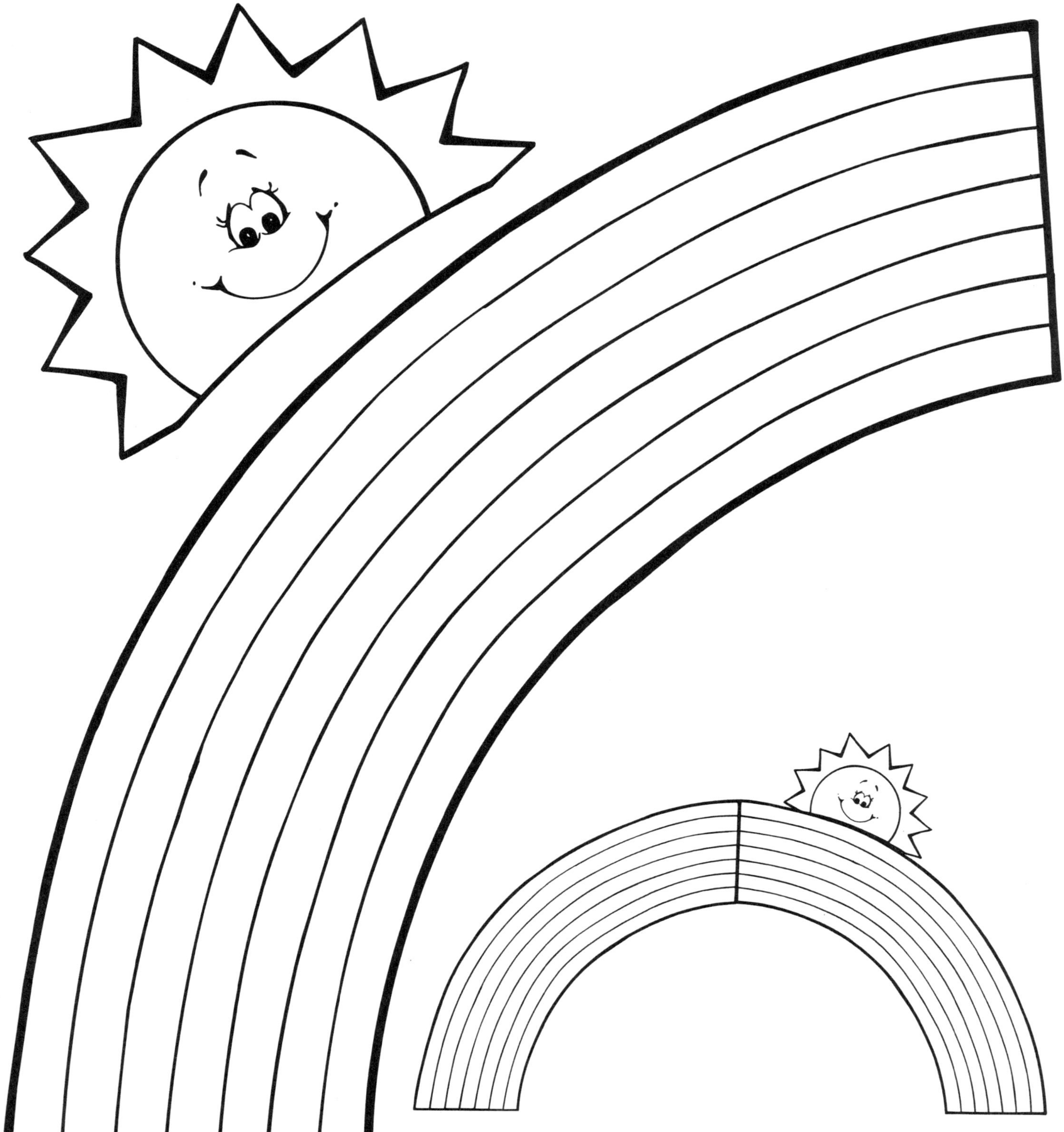

Enlarge two times. Attach to board, as above, to create rainbow.

Hot News!

". . . I am sending you to Pharaoh to bring my people the Israelites out of Egypt."
(Exodus 3:10)

This board will help the children understand what an important job God wanted Moses to do.

Materials Needed:
enlarged copy of the patterns on page 52, crayons or markers

Preparation:
Color the enlarged bush pattern green and orange and attach it to the center of the board. Place Moses near the bush. Beneath the pictures, add the title.

Directions:
Tell the children the story of "Moses and the Burning Bush" (Exodus 3:1–12). Then discuss with the children the fact that God was asking Moses to do an important job. Tell them that Moses was scared about being able to do what God asked. Talk about how God encouraged Moses and even let Moses' brother, Aaron, come along to Egypt so Moses wouldn't be so scared. Talk with the children about things they have to do that are hard. Encourage them to ask God's help with hard things they must do.

Hot News!

continued

Rules to Live By

"These are the laws you are to set before them." (Exodus 21:1)

This board provides the perfect way for the children to learn all about God's laws.

Materials Needed:

an enlarged copy of the tablets on page 54 on gray paper, one copy of the tablets per child, brightly colored paper (board background)

Preparation:

Cover the board with brightly colored paper. Attach the enlarged tablets to the board.

Directions:

Read the children the story of God giving Moses the Ten Commandments (Exodus 19:25–20:17). As you read each commandment, write it on the stone tablet in wording that the children will understand. Help the children write these same words on their small tablets to take home.

Rules to Live By

continued

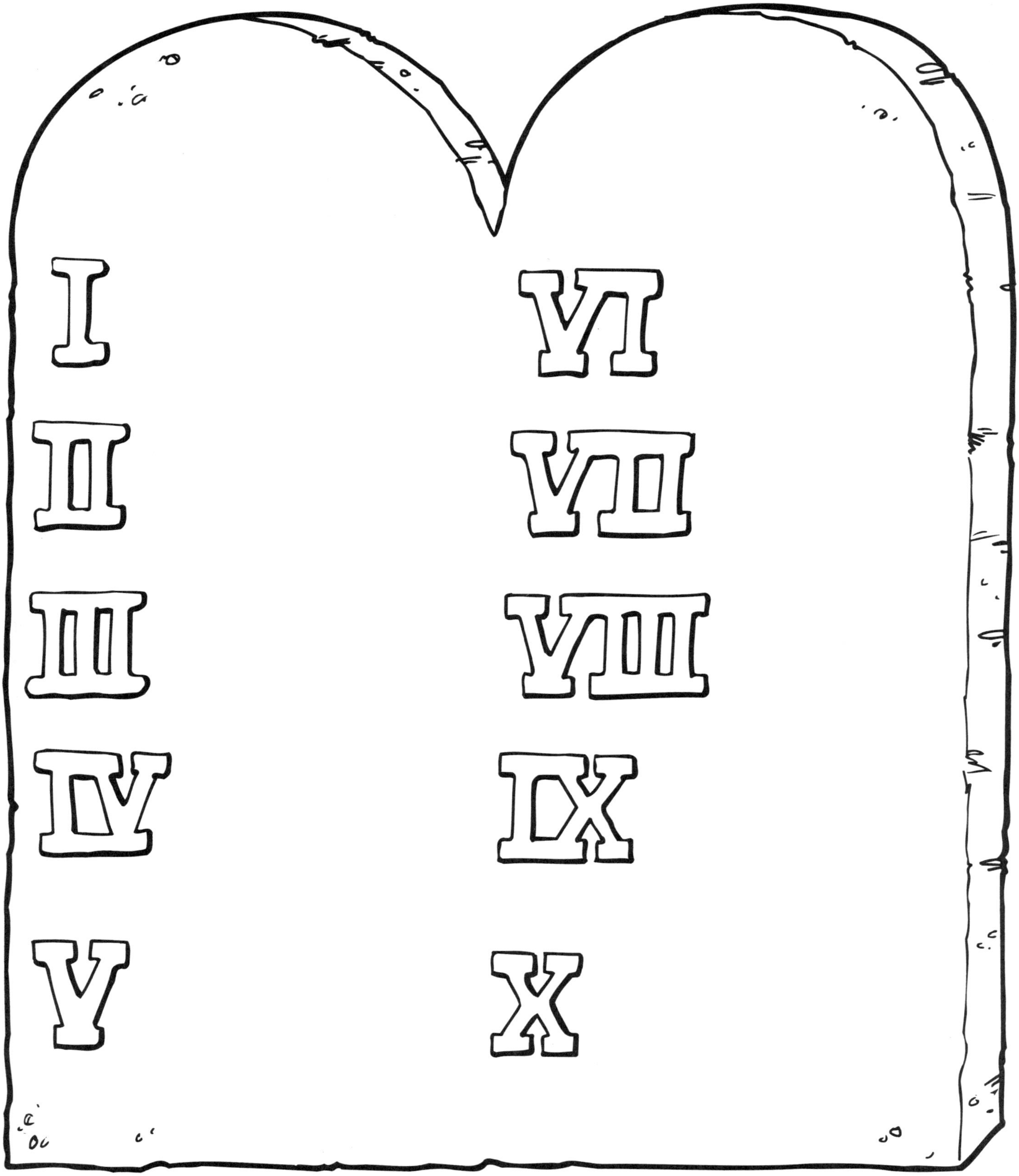

Jesus' Special Friends

"You are my friends if you do what I command." (John 16:14)

This board provides a wonderful way for the children to learn about Jesus' 12 disciples and how they helped Him.

Materials Needed:

an enlarged copy of the Jesus pattern on page 56, 12 (total) enlarged copies of the men patterns on page 56, crayons or markers, white paper (board background)

Preparation:

Cover the board with white paper. Color the 12 patterns to look like the 12 disciples. Color the Jesus pattern to look like Jesus.

Directions:

Read Mark 3:16–19 to the children. Let them give each pattern the name of one of the disciples. Arrange the pictures like a class picture. Put Jesus' picture in the center and the disciples around Him. Talk about the work the disciples did. Talk about things the children can do to show their love for Jesus.

Jesus' Special Friends

continued

A Miracle Wedding Drink

. . . "With man this is impossible, but not with God; all things are possible with God."
(Mark 10:27)

The children can learn about the first miracle Jesus performed with this board.

Materials Needed:
two enlarged copies of the jar pattern on page 58 and one copy of the jar pattern per child, light colored paper (board background), clear and red cellophane, crayons

Preparation:
Cover the board with light colored paper. Color and attach the jars to the board. The first one should be upright; the second should be tilted so that its contents are spilling out. Take a long strip of clear plastic wrap and fold it over so it is thick. Squeeze it, crinkle it, and attach it to the board so that it looks like water being poured into the upright jar. For the second jar, which is tilted, attach red cellophane, doubled and crinkled, in the same way as the clear cellophane, to make it look like wine spilling out. Write the featured verse on the bottom of the board.

Directions:
Read or tell the children the story of Jesus changing water into wine (John 2:1–11). Discuss what a miracle this is. Talk about some experiences they have had that the children think are miracles. Then give each child a jar. Let them decorate one side of their jars. On the other side, write, "Jesus can do anything." Let the children use their jars to tell their families the story of Jesus' first miracle.

A Miracle Wedding Drink

continued

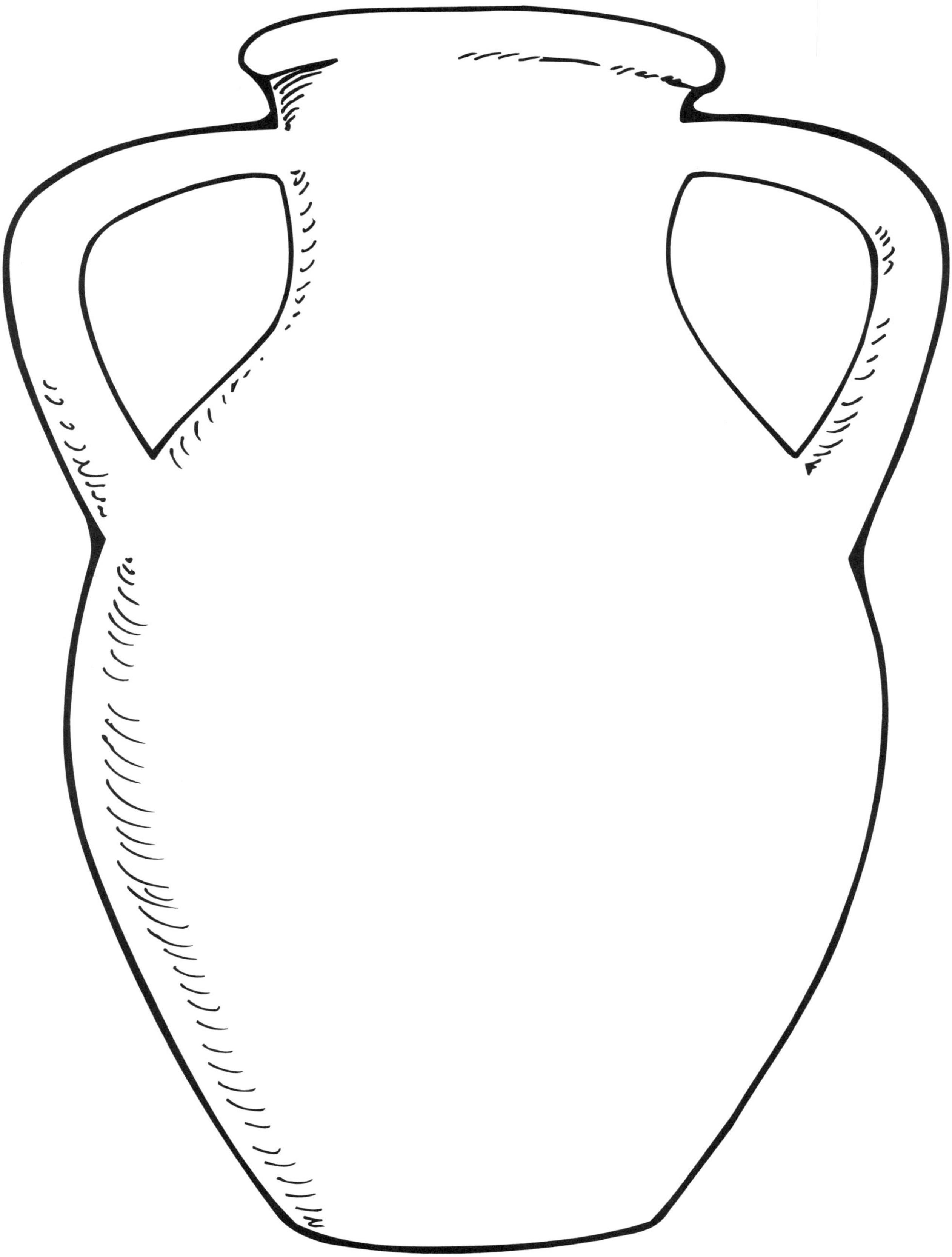

Good Soil/Bad Soil

Let the wise listen and add to their learning . . . (Proverbs 1:5)

This board emphasizes the importance of understanding God's Word and living by it.

Materials Needed:

two copies of the bird patterns on page 60; a few copies of the weak-looking plant pattern on page 60; a few copies of the healthy-looking plant pattern on page 60 for the board and one copy of one per child; gray, brown, and bright green paper (board background); seeds; glue; crayons or markers; stapler

Preparation:

Divide the board into thirds. Cover the first section in gray paper, the middle section in brown paper, and the third in bright green paper. Glue some seeds onto the board in the first section. Then staple the birds to look as though they are eating the seeds. In the middle section, attach the weak-looking plants. Then in the final section, staple the healthy-looking plants. Below the pictures, write the featured Bible verse.

Directions:

Give each child a copy of a healthy-looking plant to color. Tell them The Parable of the Sower (Matthew 13:1–23). Discuss with the children the importance of hearing God's Word, listening to it, and living by it.

Good Soil/Bad Soil

continued

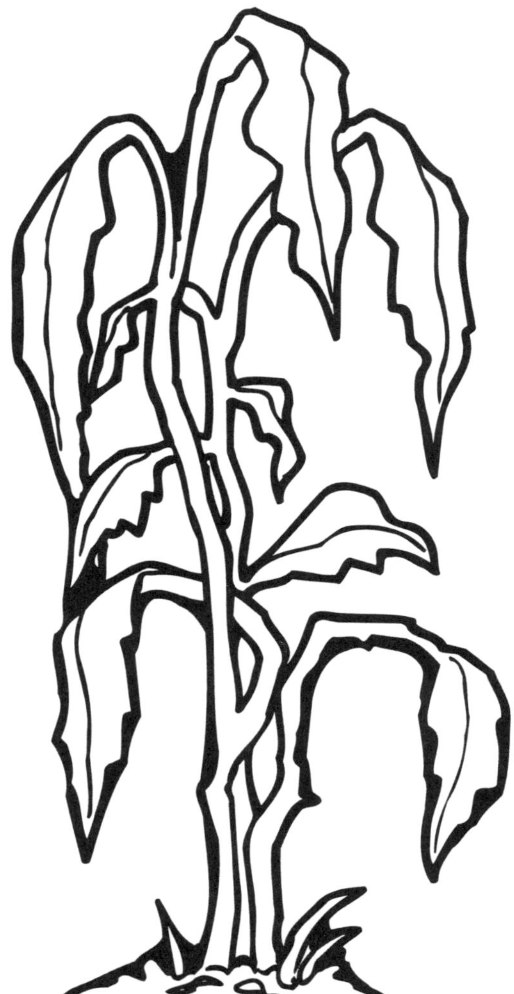

Fruit of the Spirit

But the fruit of the Spirit is love, joy, peace, patience, kindness, goodness, faithfulness, gentleness and self-control . . . (Galatians 5:22–23)

This board can help the children learn many important values all Christians need in their lives.

Materials Needed:

several enlarged copies of each fruit pattern on pages 62–63 and one copy of a fruit pattern per child, crayons or markers, green paper (board background)

Preparation:

Cover the board with green paper. Add the title (and the Bible verse, if desired). Write each fruit of the Spirit on a piece of fruit. Lightly color over them.

Directions:

Discuss the Bible verse with the children. Talk about each fruit of the Spirit and ways the children have it in their lives. Give each child a piece of fruit. Help the children write a fruit of the Spirit on their fruits, decorate them, and take them home.

Fruit of the Spirit

continued

Fruit of the Spirit

continued

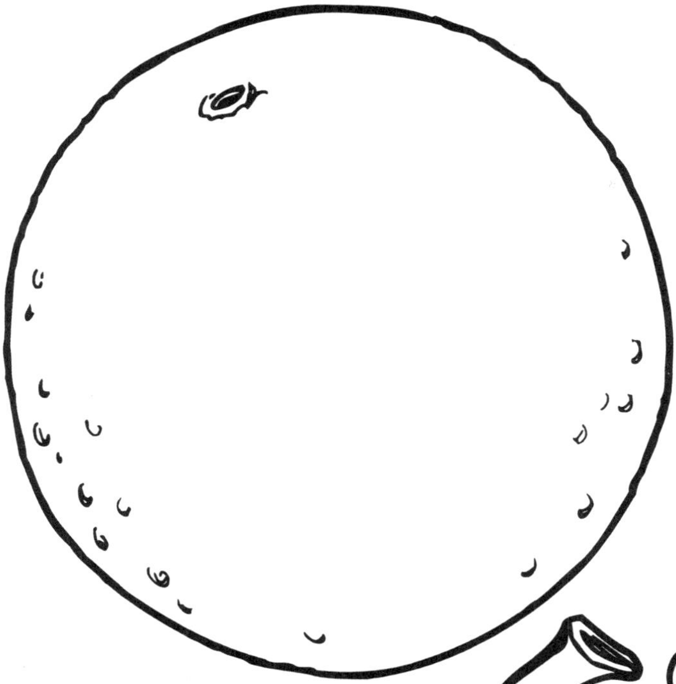

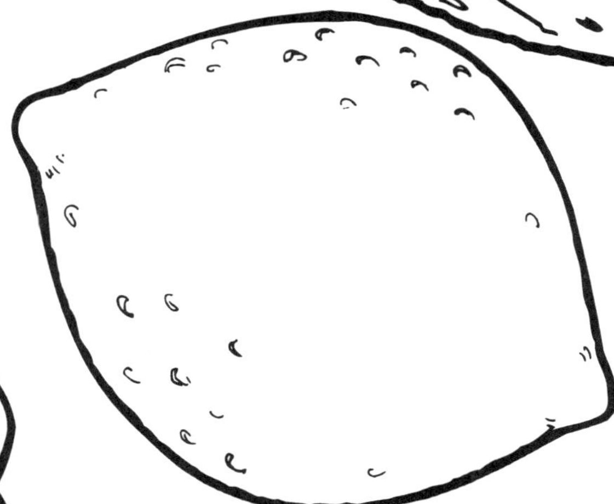

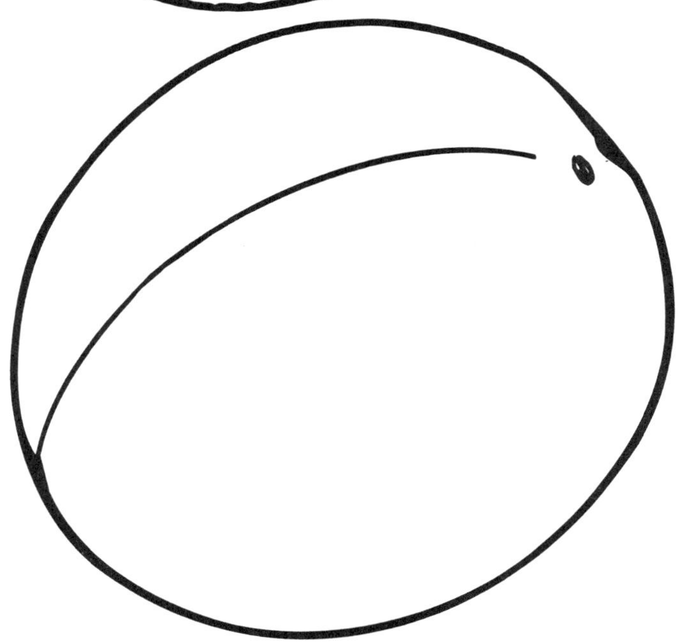

A Big Secret

. . . *She named him Moses, saying, "I drew him out of the water."* (Exodus 2:10)

The story this board teaches is a favorite of many children!

Materials Needed:

enlarged copy of the basket pattern on page 65, enlarged green copies of the reed pattern on page 65, an enlarged copy of the pattern on page 66, blue and green paper (board background)

Preparation:

Cover the bottom of the board with blue paper. Cover the top of the board with green paper. Add the title. Attach the basket to the water. Line the river with the reeds and bend them slightly so they stick out from the board. Color and hide the Miriam pattern in the reeds so she can see the basket.

Directions:

Tell the children the story of Moses' mother putting him in the basket to protect him from Pharaoh (Exodus 2:1–10). Discuss how mean Pharaoh was to God's people. See if the children can tell you of other meanness going on in our world today. Say a prayer together asking God to help people be nice to each other.

A Big Secret

continued

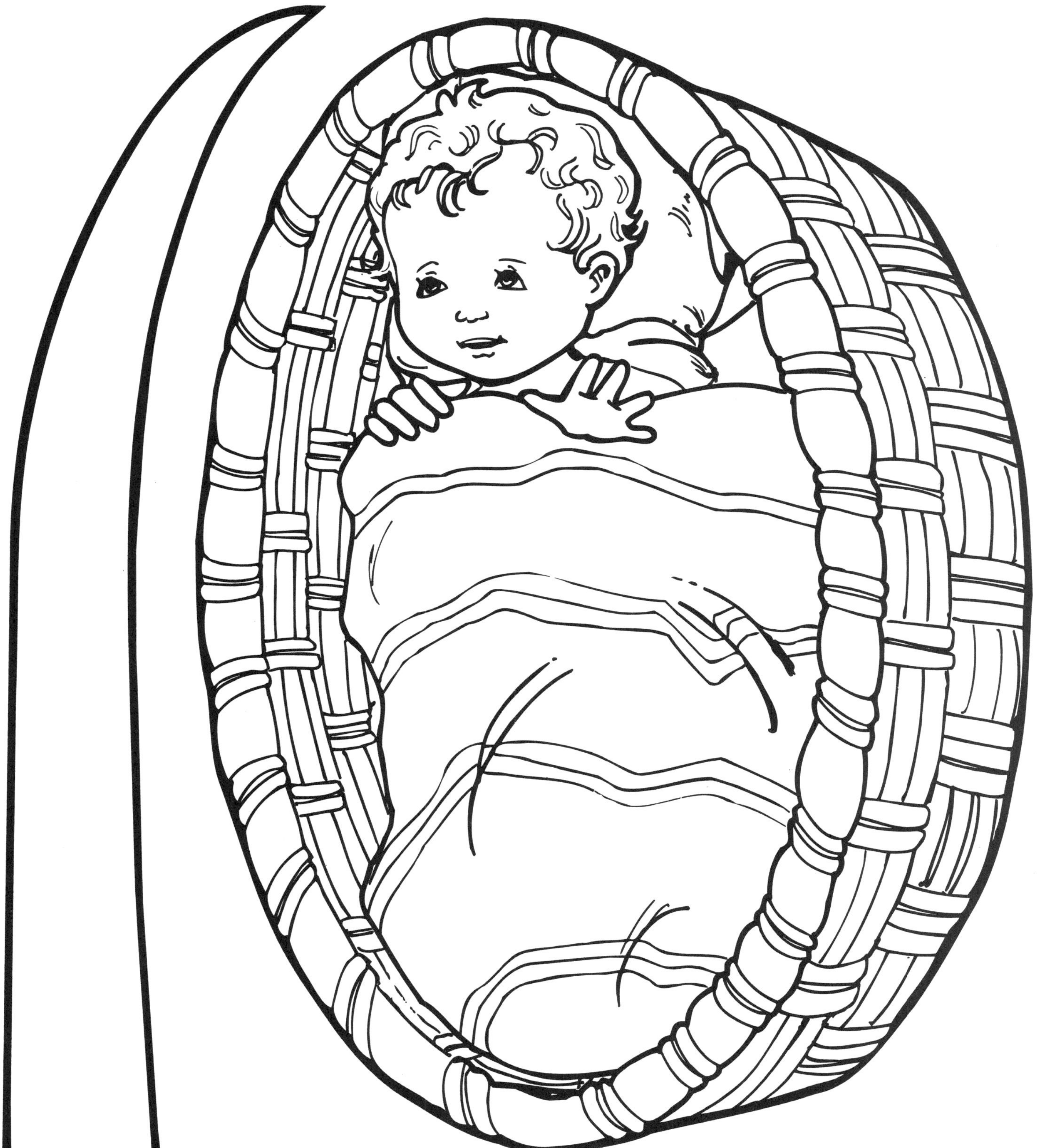

A Big Secret

continued

The Fiery Furnace

My help comes from the Lord, the Maker of heaven and earth. (Psalm 121:2)

This board is a wonderful way to teach the children how God protects His loved ones.

Materials Needed:

enlarged copies of the flame pattern on page 68 on red and orange paper, an enlarged copy of the men patterns on page 69, an enlarged copy of the angel pattern on page 68, white and black paper (board background), stapler

Preparation:

Cover the top of the board with white paper and the bottom with black paper. Write the featured Bible verse on the bottom of the board. Staple the flames across the board so that eventually, they can be pulled back to show what's behind them. Staple the three men and the angel behind some of the flames and gently fold the flames back so the men and the angel can't be seen.

Directions:

Tell the children the story of Shadrach, Meshach, and Abednego in the fiery furnace (Daniel 3). As you tell the story, pull the flames back to reveal the men and the angel underneath. Discuss with the children ways the Lord protects them, too.

The Fiery Furnace

continued

The Fiery Furnace

continued

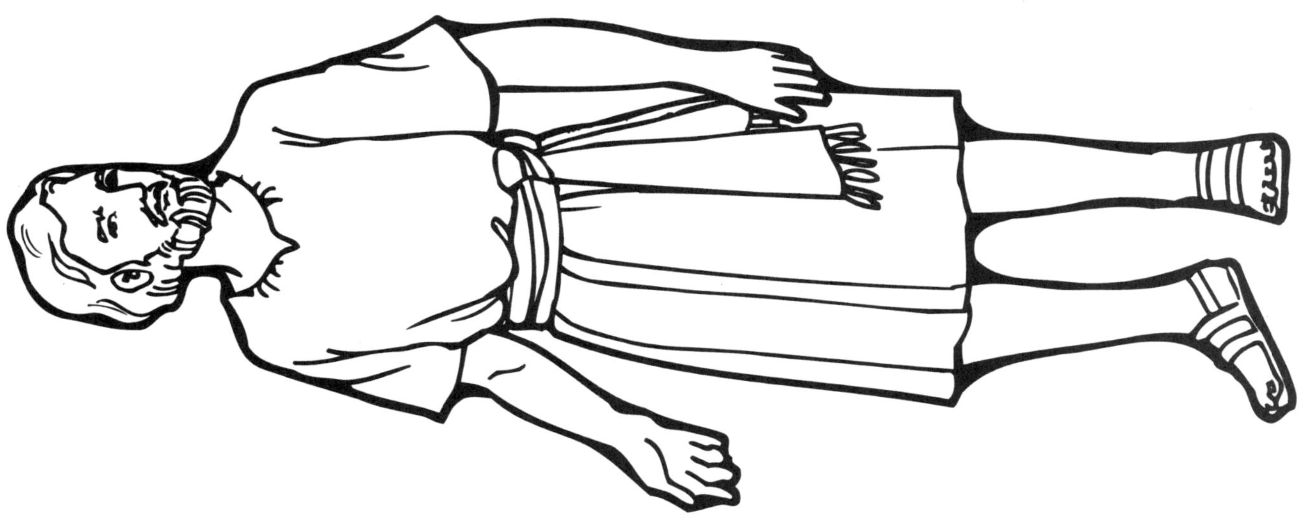

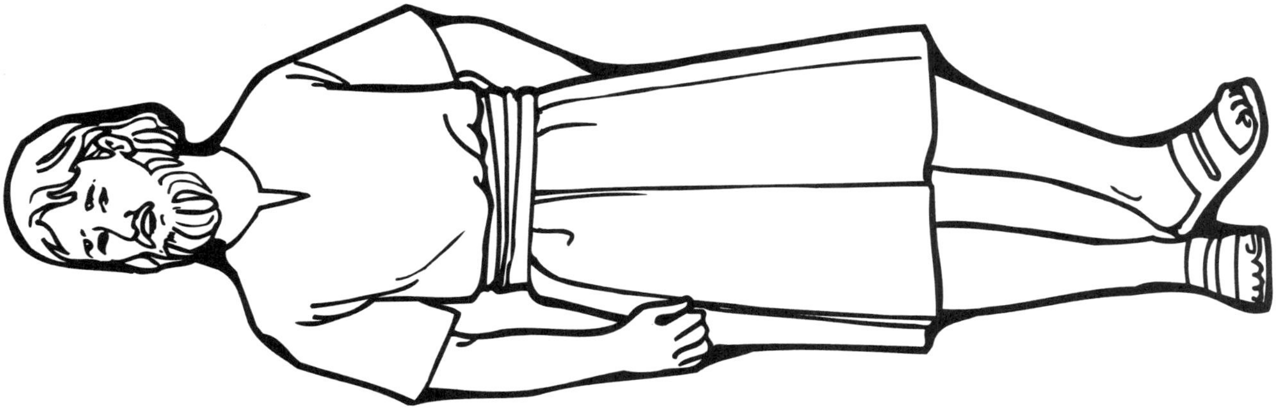

Daniel in the Lions' Den

God is our refuge and strength, an ever-present help in trouble. (Psalm 46:1)

What a wonderful story all children love—and a wonderful board to help you tell it!

Materials Needed:

an enlarged copy of the Daniel pattern on page 71, an enlarged copy of the lion and rock patterns on pages 71–72, one copy of a lion pattern for each child, gray paper (board background), crayons or markers

Preparation:

Cover the board with gray paper. Color Daniel and the enlarged lions. Outline the rocks in dark gray or black. Attach everything to the board. Add the featured Bible verse under the picture.

Directions:

Tell the children the story of God protecting Daniel (Daniel 6). Give each child a lion. Let the children color their lions and write on them a way that God protects them.

Daniel in the Lions' Den

continued

Daniel in the Lions' Den

continued

The Crucifixion

God demonstrates his own love for us in this: While we were still sinners, Christ died for us. (Romans 5:8)

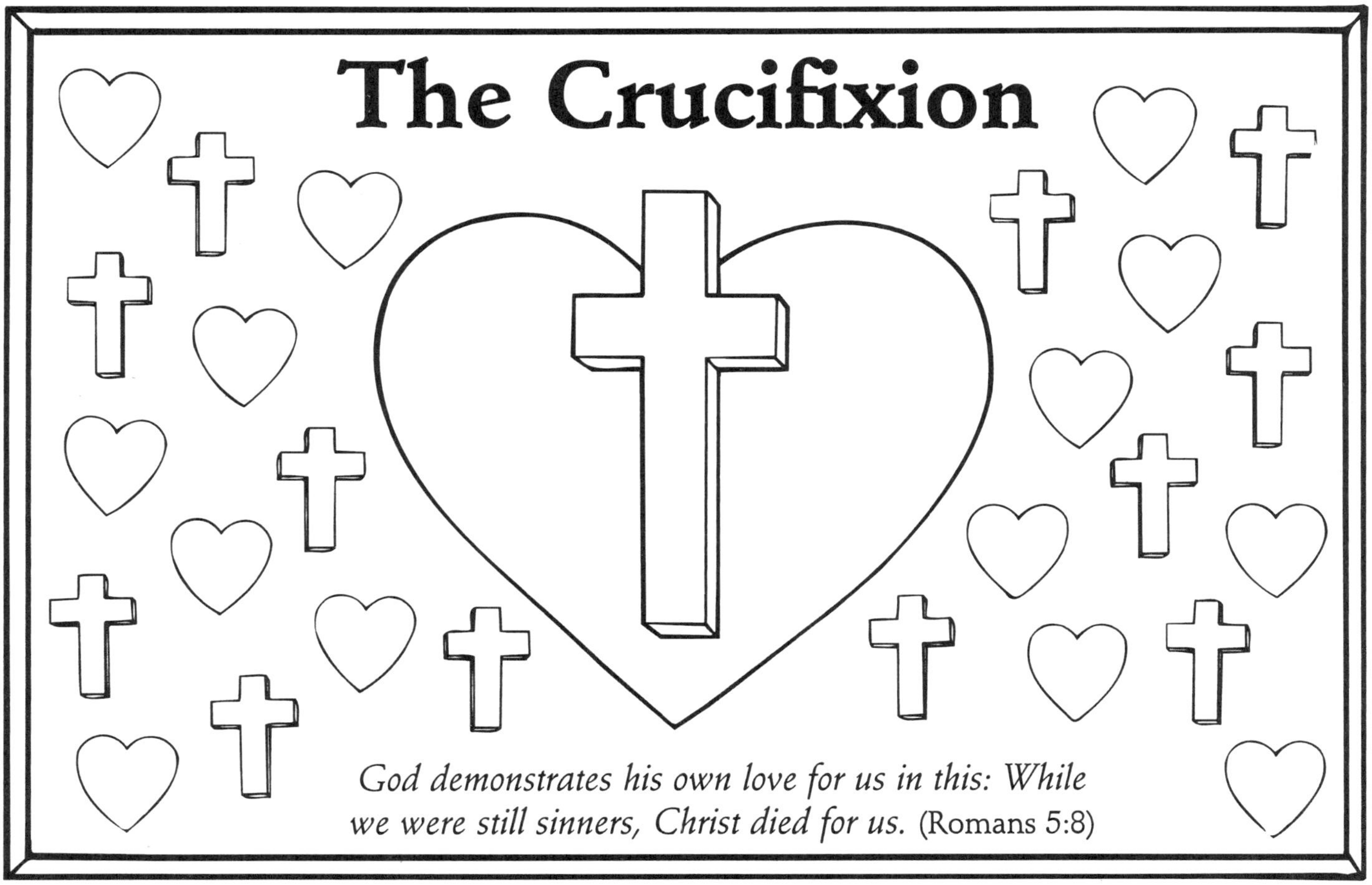

This board provides a way for you to explain to the children the great love God has for us—He sent His only Son to die for us.

Materials Needed:

an enlarged copy of the pattern on page 74 (large enough to fill the center of the board), several copies of the heart and cross patterns on page 75, light colored paper (board background)

Preparation:

Cover the board with light colored paper. Attach the cross/heart picture to the center of the board. Attach the small crosses and hearts around it. (The children could color the crosses and hearts and even write short prayers on them if you like.) Below the cross/heart, write the featured Bible verse.

Directions:

Read the children the story of the crucifixion and discuss it with them (John 19:16–37). Christ did so much for us; ask the children what they can do for Him.

The Crucifixion

continued

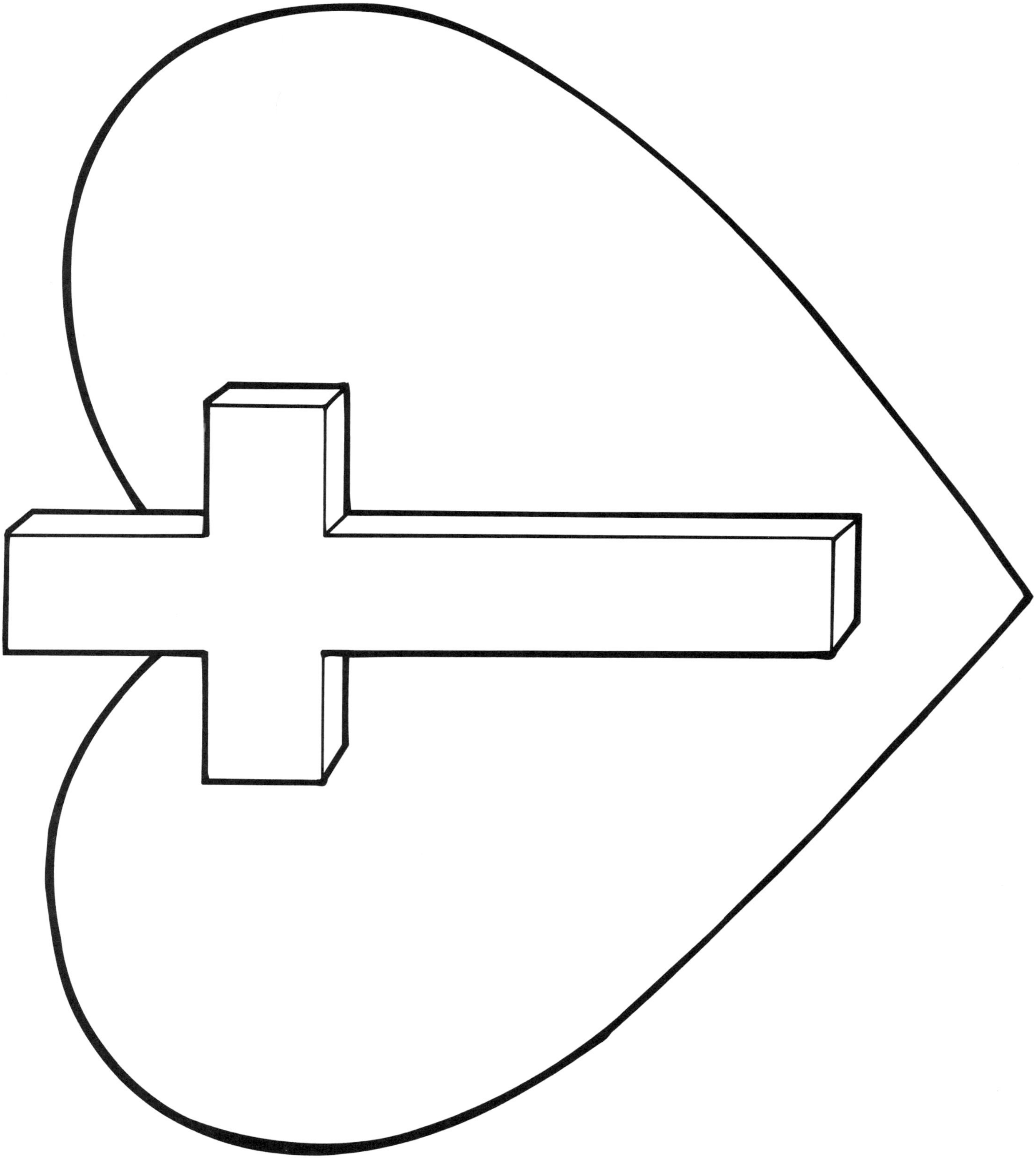

Food for Elijah

continued

Do Unto Others

"Do to others as you would have them do to you." (Luke 6:31)

This board features a Bible verse everyone needs to know!

Materials Needed:
an enlarged copy of the letters on pages 79–80 (the title should fill the board), bright paper (board background), 3" x 5" cards

Preparation:
Cover the board with bright paper. Attach the title to the board.

Directions:
Ask the children for one word descriptions of ways they like to be treated and ways in which they can treat others. Write these words on 3" x 5" cards. Attach them randomly around the title.

Do Unto Others

continued

Do Unto Others

continued

God Is Love

. . . God is love . . . (1 John 4:16)

What a wonderful Bible verse the children should memorize! This board will be filled with God's love when it is done.

Materials Needed:

various enlarged sizes of the heart patterns on page 82, white paper (board background), red and pink crayons

Preparation:

Cover the board with white paper. Write the verse in large letters in the center of the board.

Directions:

Ask the children to name ways that God shows love to them. Write their responses on the hearts. Let the children lightly color over the hearts. Attach the hearts randomly around the verse on the board.

God Is Love

continued

You Are the Salt

"You are the salt of the earth . . ." (Matthew 5:13)

This board will help the children better understand the important role each of them has on earth.

Materials Needed:

enlarged copies of the patterns on pages 84–85, dark blue paper (board background), scissors (optional: individual pictures of the children)

Preparation:

Cover the board with dark blue paper. Write the featured Bible verse as a title. Attach the salt shaker to the upper left corner of the board, tipping it as if salt is spilling out. On the bottom, attach the earth pattern you have colored. Then, pouring from the salt shaker, attach either individual pictures of the children or their names, written out individually. Color and randomly attach the star patterns.

Directions:

Explain to the children what being the salt of the earth means (salt adds flavor, and therefore, each child adds "flavor" to the earth with his or her own unique qualities). Ask each child to tell something that makes him or her unique or special.

You Are the Salt

continued

You Are the Salt

continued

Watch Your Language

If anyone considers himself religious and yet does not keep a tight rein on his tongue, he deceives himself . . . (James 1:26)

This board is a great way to remind the children to say only kind things.

Materials Needed:

a copy of page 87 for each child, bright red paper (board background), crayons or markers

Preparation:

Cover the board with bright red paper. Write the title or the featured Bible verse on the board.

Directions:

Discuss the Bible verse with the children. Talk about how it is important to say only kind things. Then give each child a copy of page 87. Let the children draw features and hair to resemble themselves and write something nice in their speech bubbles. Attach them all over the board.

Watch Your Language

continued

Light Your World

"You are the light of the world . . ." (Matthew 5:14)

This is a great way to help the children understand that they can show God's love to others by living according to His Word.

Materials Needed:

enlarged copies of the patterns on page 89 on bright yellow and orange paper, one copy of one of the light patterns on page 89 per child, black or dark blue paper (board background), crayons or markers

Preparation:

Cover the board with black or dark blue paper. Add the title. Scatter the various enlarged light patterns on the dark board.

Directions:

Read and discuss Matthew 5:14–16 with the children. Talk with the children about being lights in the world. Explain to them how they can show God's love to others by how they live in the world. Give each child one of the lights to decorate and take home as a reminder.

Light Your World

continued

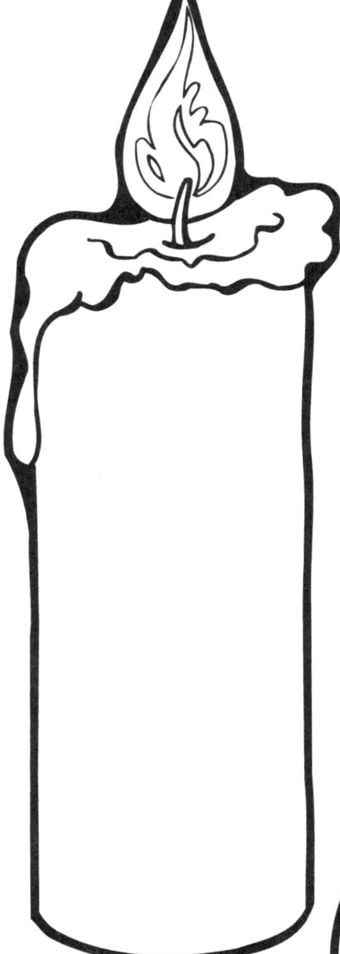

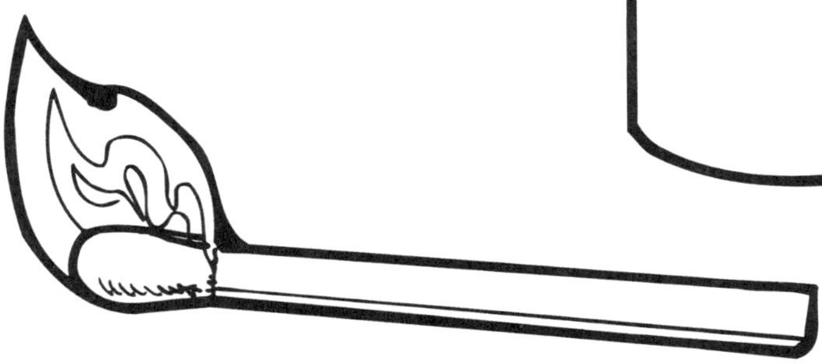

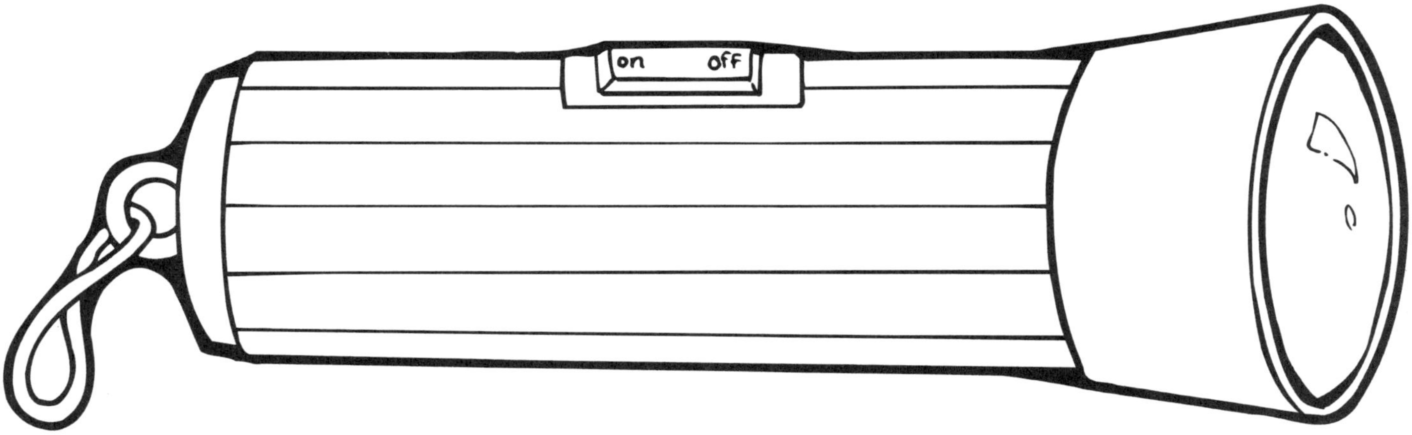

Give Your Worries Away

Cast all your anxiety on him because he cares for you. (1 Peter 5:7)

What a wonderful way to encourage the children to turn to God with their concerns.

Materials Needed:

an enlarged copy of the patterns on pages 91–92, yellow paper (board background), 3" x 5" cards, construction paper

Preparation:

Cover the board with yellow paper. Attach colored pictures of the boy and girl. Add a large construction paper cross to the center. Then add the featured Bible verse and title.

Directions:

Discuss 1 Peter 5:7 with the children. Tell them that they can talk to God about anything that is bothering them and He will listen to them. Have the children name prayer requests. Write each request on a 3" x 5" card. Attach these to the board. If there are not too many requests, you could attach them on the cross.

Give Your Worries Away

continued

Give Your Worries Away

continued

First Love

We love because he first loved us. (1 John 4:19)

The theme of this board is easy for the children to understand. Without Jesus' love and guidance, it would be hard to share our love with others.

Materials Needed:

an enlarged copy of the Jesus pattern on page 94; soft colored paper (board background); one photograph of each child or 3" x 5" cards, each containing one of the children's names

Preparation:

Cover the board with soft colored paper. Attach the picture of Jesus to the center. Around His picture, attach pictures (or names) of the children. Below the pictures, write the featured Bible verse.

Directions:

Discuss the featured Bible verse with the children. Talk with the children about the many ways we know Jesus loves us.

First Love

continued

A Hidden Surprise

I have hidden your word in my heart that I might not sin against you. (Psalm 119:11)

This is a wonderful way to help the children learn that God lives in their hearts, and by remembering this, they can try to avoid sin.

Materials Needed:

one enlarged heart using the pattern on page 96 and one heart pattern (of different sizes) per child, one copy of the Bible pattern on page 96 (this will fit inside a "door" you cut in the largest heart), pink paper (board background), crayons or markers, scissors

Preparation:

Cover the board with pink paper. Cut a "door" that can be opened in the largest heart pattern. Attach this heart to the board. Open the door and hide the Bible pattern behind it. Add the featured Bible verse. Have the children decorate their hearts and attach them to the board.

Directions:

Discuss Psalm 119:11 with the children. Help them understand that if they remember that God's love and Word lives in their hearts, it will be easier for them to do what is right and avoid sin. Then open the door to reveal what is behind the door.

A Hidden Surprise

continued

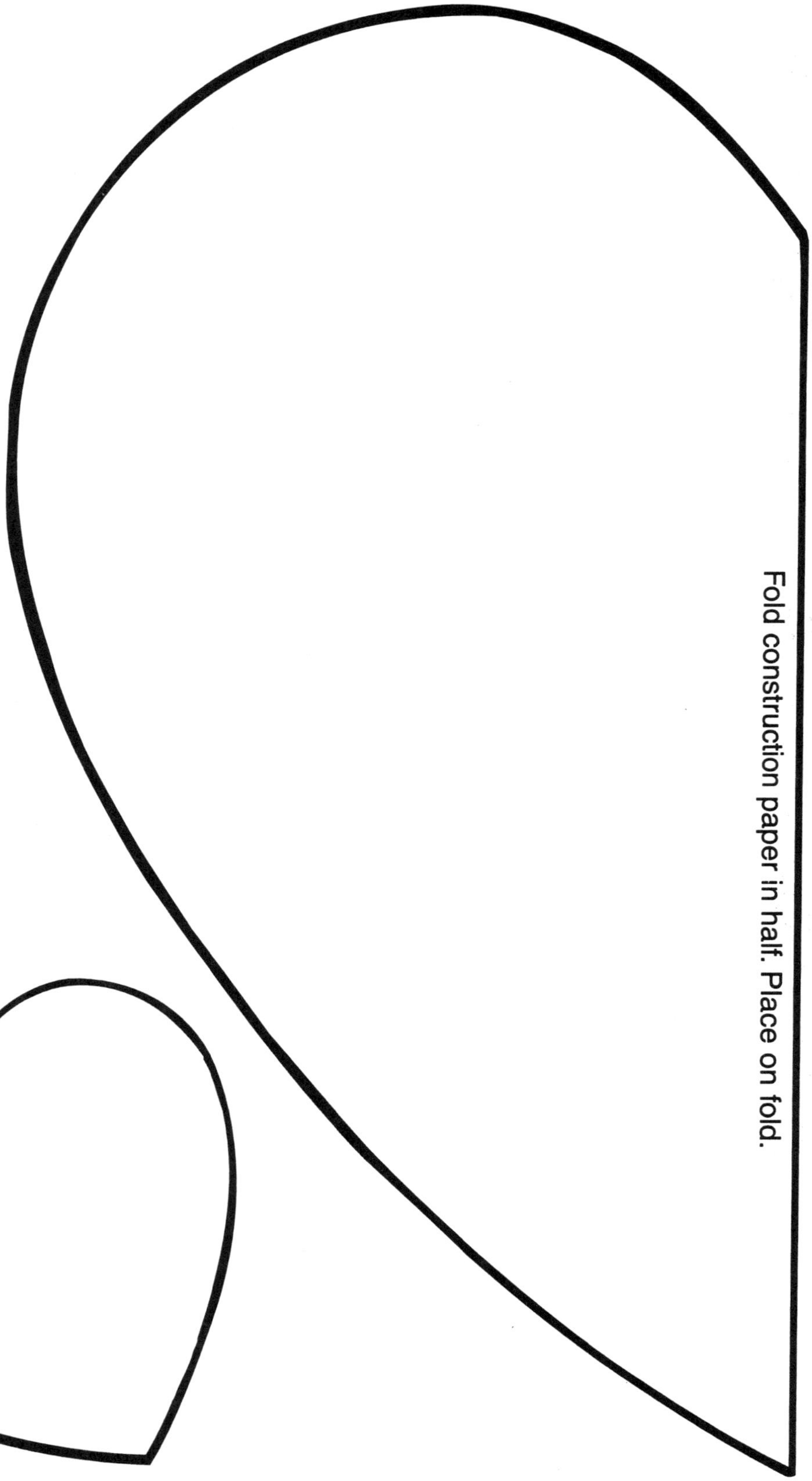